love changes
everything

love changes
everything

seven remarkable real-life stories

muthena paul alkazraji

Scripture Union, 207–209 Queensway, Bletchley, MK2 2EB, England.
Email: info@scriptureunion.org.uk
Web site: www.scriptureunion.org.uk

ISBN 1 85999 306 0

Scriptures quoted from the Good News Bible published by The Bible
Societies / HarperCollins Publishers Limited, UK, © American Bible
Society, 1966, 1971, 1976, 1992.

British Library Cataloguing-in-Publication Data
A catalogue record for this book is available from the British Library.

Photographs by Muthena Paul Alkazraji.
Cover design by Jon Birch.
Printed and bound in Great Britain by Cox & Wyman Ltd.

CONTENTS

Thanks to Andew Clark at Scripture Union for the backing, Jon Birch for the design and time, Claire and Hobbsy for their comments, Simon Kay for the introduction, Mum for the constant support and Liz Russell for being a true sister.

Also thanks to Bob, Cherie, Ernesto, 'Sarah' (our kid), Catherine, Robin and Hans for agreeing to tell me their stories.

PREFACE

My own story is not one that I have included here. However, for me my experience was no less a transformation than that demonstrated in the lives of the people you will meet in these pages. I too know that the love of Christ has rescued me. This rescue operation continues daily, gently and steadily.

Here you will read the stories, among others, of a man whose crime might elicit little sympathy from most of us; a man mysteriously delivered from political oppression in Latin America and facing a new life in unfamiliar surroundings; and a woman whose healing may seem like a fairy-tale, only it is true.

For many people the road to faith takes place over time and without great drama. Often, however, it is when our comfortable route through life is disrupted, when the securities that precariously shore us up are taken away, or when our fragility is revealed to us, that we face our need of God's saving love head on. Jesus Christ is waiting for us now. He calls us to take a step forward to meet him.

Hans Segers

Chapter 1

HANS: PENALTY SAVIOUR

Hans Segers rummages through the garage of his St Albans home for his crumpled old Wolverhampton Wanderers shirt. In a carrier bag he finds the precious top he wore on the day of the FA Cup sixth round against Leeds United in 1998, when he made a crucial last-minute penalty save to take Wolves through to the semi-final. Hans currently coaches Tottenham Hotspur's first team goalies, and has to leave for White Hart Lane in half an hour. 'We've got a match against Chelsea on SKY TV this evening.' He dons the shirt quickly for a photograph, and we head back to the kitchen where his wife, Astrid, has been preparing his dinner.

Hans and Astrid have been married for fourteen years, but have known each other since they were young teenagers in Holland. Today there is a relaxed ease between them, but back in the summer of 1994, when all was well on the pitch for Hans (then Wimbledon FC's goalkeeper) things had reached a critical point at home. 'Me and my wife were leading separate lives. We were drifting away from each other, and at one stage my suitcase was virtually outside the door. She couldn't cope with my behaviour – I was arrogant and very difficult to live with. You could say that I was a bit of a Jack the lad.

'We'd start to talk about things and, if I didn't agree,

9

I'd close the door behind me, take the car and I was off. I'd get my clubs and I'd go play golf – or it was nights out with the boys.' Hans was largely preoccupied with the pleasures and privileges of being a professional soccer player on a good income. 'I was enjoying life and misusing it one way or another.'

At the time, Astrid was working as a part-time hairdresser. One afternoon she began a conversation with one of her clients as she trimmed her hair. 'Astrid found that she felt quite comfortable being open with this lady, and she started talking about the problems in our marriage. The woman showed a lot of warmth and Astrid asked her if by any chance she was a Christian. She said, "Yes, actually I am", and she invited Astrid along to one of her home-group meetings. Astrid really enjoyed it, and one or two weeks after that she made a commitment. At the time, though, I didn't know anything about it.'

One day Hans noticed his wife reading a particularly large book. 'Astrid is not one of the biggest readers in the world – apart from magazines. I couldn't see what it was, as she had put wrapping paper around it! I knew afterwards that she was trying to hide that she was reading the Bible.'

Hans had his own particular perception of people who attend church. 'I thought they were sad – people with problems, lunatics, "light-bulb changers".' He grins, raising both hands into the air to quickly twiddle two imaginary light bulbs loose, in mock Pentecostal fervour. 'But, as the weeks went by, I saw this difference in Astrid. All of a sudden, she started to be really nice to me – she was warm and soft. I thought, *What is going on here, then?* She seemed able to forgive the things I'd done, and that made me really interested.'

Despite the drift in his relationship with Astrid, Hans genuinely wanted to make it work. 'One day Astrid came up to me and told me that the only way our marriage would survive was if I became a Christian. I started laughing. She said that I had to ask Jesus Christ into my life. I thought, *What has he got to do with it? It's just us two and nobody else.* I left it like that.'

Shortly afterwards, Hans decided that he should try to talk over the situation with Astrid's brother, Adrie, who was a Baptist minister, and his wife, Petra. They lived near Antwerp in Belgium. 'Something said to me, "Hans, you have to go to Belgium." I know now where that thought came from.' He put this to Astrid. 'She said it was an answer to prayer and broke down crying.' They took the Euro-Tunnel across the Channel, then drove the hour-and-a-half to the town where Hans's in-laws lived. 'On the way there, I was thinking that I just wanted to get my marriage back on the rails – that was all I wanted. I was desperate for some help.'

In Adrie and Petra's living room, the subject turned to the Christian faith. 'We talked from seven till eleven in the evening. We talked and talked, and a few tears were flowing. What stands out in my mind was, as Adrie put it, if I made a commitment to Christ he was able to forgive all my sins, because I had loads … loads. I found it such an amazing thing that someone could forgive all the things I'd done.' A sense of guilt began to surface in Hans. 'There are things in the past that you try to forget, but you have to live with. They are like a barrier in your life – things you carry on your shoulders everywhere you go. The biggest thing for me was what I'd done to Astrid and the children – neglecting them.'

Hans decided he would take the step. 'That night I

went down on my knees and asked the Lord to come into my heart and lead my life. I was so desperate. I was in such a state. I was going to do anything to get my marriage back on the rails.' He felt a deep sense of peace, though he didn't sleep very well that night! 'I was so happy, I was wide awake. Astrid and me talked all through the night. She was just so glad that I'd made a commitment.' Adrie assured him of his place in heaven. 'I felt like I'd won the jackpot, the biggest jackpot we can ever have. I was like a real happy chappy.'

They returned to their home in the UK the following day, then shortly began attending services in the nearby village. Hans's relationship with Astrid began to improve. 'I began to spend more time with the family, and we did things together that we hadn't done before. I think my self-control was a lot better than it had been – I was getting angry less quickly. Astrid said I was a lot softer and kinder. Other people said so, too.' Despite these things, however, Hans's heart wasn't in his new-found faith. He'd kept his marriage on track and he felt that he'd secured eternal life, but... 'My faith wasn't strong towards God. I'd got what I wanted and I thought, *That'll do me.*'

Seven months later, in March 1995, Hampshire detectives knocked on Hans's door at six o'clock in the morning. In a series of simultaneous early morning raids, Hans, Southampton goalkeeper Bruce Grobbelaar, Aston Villa striker John Fashanu, and Malaysian businessman Richard Lim were arrested on suspicion of conspiracy to influence the outcome of soccer matches for a Far Eastern betting syndicate. The arrests hit the headlines.

Hans had indeed taken payments from Richard Lim, but for acting as a pundit and forecasting the outcome of matches in the Dutch Football League. He had never attempted to swing a match in which he played for a bribe – the criminal charge that was to be levelled at himself, Grobbelaar and Fashanu. However, at Eastlea police station that day, in the heat of the moment, Hans fabricated a story about the source of some of his money, saying it was the proceeds from crime in his youth, fearing other consequences. This did not help his case and he regrets it. He had also become aware, after having begun forecasting for Lim, that this was contrary to the Football Association's rules. And he had neglected to pay tax. These were his offences – not attempted match-swinging.

'On the afternoon of the day of my arrest, my church minister was straight on the phone to the police station. He prayed over the phone and really encouraged me. He prayed for strength, saying, "Don't worry. God won't let you down." After I came out of the station, I went to the church on the Sunday. The people there didn't know if I was guilty or not, but they didn't judge me. They were just there for me and my family. This was so special, because around the country people were reading the papers and pointing the finger at you, assuming you were guilty.'

Hans and his co-defendants were to endure a protracted two-and-a-half year wait before the legal process would reach its conclusion. The first hearing, at Winchester Crown Court, didn't begin until January 1997. After three months, the jury found they could not reach a majority verdict on any of the defendants, and the case went to a retrial. The second hearing began in Winchester that June.

'Throughout the trials, our best friends, Linda and Graham, prayed every Sunday evening for all the events in the coming week, and Graham came along to give me moral support.' Hans also took strength from passages of scripture specially given to him by members of his church. 'A lot of them said, "The Lord will look after you, no matter how bad the situation gets." I had a feeling from then onwards that the Lord was telling me, "Don't worry. At the end of the journey you'll come out as a winner." That got me through the trial and the times of preparation, sitting together with my defence team.'

One specific piece of Old Testament Scripture was given to him the day before he took the stand in the second trial: 'You will not have to fight this battle. Just take up your positions and wait; you will see the Lord give you victory .... Do not hesitate or be afraid. Go out to battle, and the Lord will be with you!'

Hans sensed that God was going to help him find the words with which to refute the prosecution. 'When it was my turn to go into the witness box, it was such a frightening experience, but I coped really well – people remarked on that. It was as if the Lord was putting the words into my mouth. All of the defence teams came up to me, so did John Fashanu and said, "Hans, you were unbelievable. You just brushed them aside." And English isn't even my first language.' Hans tried to encourage his co-defendants as best he could. 'In the low times, I think I was the only one who was still cheerful. I think they knew where I got it from.'

There were further signs of a special presence with both Astrid and himself. 'Our biggest fear was for our children, that they would be stared at and bullied, so we said a lot of prayers for them. The amazing thing was that they had no trouble at all at school. And you know how children are – they can be very nasty to each other.'

During this second trial, Hans received a letter from his solicitor saying that his QC would have to stop working because of his health. 'He suffered from very high blood pressure – he was drinking and smoking – and he could hardly speak.' They considered replacing him, but two years into the case, with 10,000 pages of evidence to go through, it would have been a severe set-back. 'We spoke to the junior barrister about it, and I saw his face turn white. It was such a high-profile case.' Two days before the QC was due to sum up in Hans's defence, his voice was in a terrible condition. 'We got together on the Wednesday night and prayed and prayed. Come the Friday morning, he stood up and addressed the judge and members of the jury without any microphone, loud and clear. I had tears in my eyes.'

Hans also believes that God has a sense of humour. 'On one occasion, we had prayed that, when the prosecution started summing up, they would be fair and square and not try to mislead the jury. In the event, after three hours of the prosecutor's address, a policeman tapped on his shoulder and said he'd heard hardly anything. Apparently the microphones hadn't been working. He asked the judge to ask the members of the jury if they wanted to hear it again. The jury said, "No thank you."

Late on a Thursday afternoon in August, after the jury had been out for four days, the foreman was asked if he had reached a verdict, and the reply was affirmative. 'My legs started trembling – they were like jelly. *After two and a half years*, I thought, *at last we've got a verdict*. First, "Richard, not guilty. John, not guilty. Hans, not guilty..." I could hear Astrid screaming on the balcony. It was such a great moment.'

The Football Association hearing followed in December that year. Hans pleaded guilty to breaching FA rules on match forecasting for Richard Lim. He was fined, but a playing ban was suspended. He was free to continue his professional career.

Hans is frank about how he would have dealt with all that was ahead of him without his deepening awareness of God's presence. 'I think I wouldn't be in this country. I could have disappeared – easily. I had the opportunity and, without God, I probably would have done it. I couldn't have faced the trials, the hassle and the media. I wouldn't have been able to cope without my faith – the pressure was so intense. But, with God, I was able to face everything thrown at me. And I saw the evidence of prayers answered in that court case.'

In the April following the FA hearing, Hans experienced what is perhaps his most treasured professional moment. 'I got the opportunity to play in the FA Cup quarter-finals against Leeds United away. We were one-nil up and two minutes before the end, Leeds got a penalty. Jimmy Floyd Hasselbaink picked up the ball and went to the spot, and I went back to my line. I just closed my eyes. I was thinking about the Lord and I said, "Lord, make me a hero again." Then I got two visions of penalties Hasselbaink had taken before, and both of them went towards my left. I made my mind up that, as soon as he shot, I'd go to my left. He shot to my left and I saved it. I was half-panicking because the ball was still in play and I was trying to organise the defence, but then the final whistle went and I thought, *What a relief*. And I just thanked God.'

The next day the papers and the television were full of it. 'I was known again as Hans Segers the goalkeeper, rather than Hans Segers from the court case. For my children, I was back in the headlines for the right reasons. It was such a great feeling. God rewarded me with that. I'll never forget the things he has done for me.'

Bob

Chapter 2

BOB: 'ALL MY LIFE I HAVE BEEN LOOKING FOR LOVE...'

Today Bob is enjoying his work as a driver. Having just left National Express coaches to join a private West Country firm, he is looking forward to doing the type of work he has always hoped for: tours and continental work to France, Italy and Scandinavia. 'I can get out and see a bit of the world,' he enthuses. The house he rents is a modern three-bedroom semi, which he and others have recently furbished with creature comforts. The light from a new large-screen colour TV illuminates the pictures on the walls of his living room: pictures of gleaming articulated trucks, an Alsatian dog sitting alert, and Christ behind the bars of a prison.

Bob's story begins when he was a boy. 'I was rejected by my parents. My mother lost a little girl before me, and it really affected her. She didn't really want me – she wanted a girl more than anything else. I wasn't allowed to have friends round and I would get shut out and wander the streets. I ended up being bullied at school and stealing from my parents to buy friendship. All my life I have been looking for love...'

Many things have helped rebuild Bob's life, but his second wife and the children of their marriage do not live here. It is a reconciliation he still prays for. 'I accept responsibility for what I've done. I know I've deeply hurt her and the kids.'

An incident back in November 1993 broke up Bob's family. His marriage had been 'having its ups and downs'. He was living in a council house and had irregular work driving lorries for an agency. 'I couldn't seem to settle in any job.' He and his wife were working up to eighteen hours a day and they had debts they were struggling to repay. They were both tired and irritable much of the time, and when their four children played up, Bob's handling of them caused further arguments. 'My biggest problem was that I couldn't show the children any affection. But I was never shown it by my parents – I was brought up by the rule of the stick and belt. For his wife and himself, their time in bed at night became their only time together. However, his approaches for attention and affection were rebuffed; he felt pushed out and lonely. His wife did, too. One morning the situation escalated. 'It ended up in one big, mighty row.' Crockery got broken and their son was hurt in the crossfire. In a fit of frustration and rage, Bob put his hands round his wife's neck and began to strangle her. Fortunately, he blacked out before causing serious physical damage. Later, when he came round, they had sex.

At lunchtime the following day Bob was arrested. He was taken to a nearby police station and charged with ABH (Actual Bodily Harm). From there he was sent to Horfield Prison on remand. 'It was a big shock. I'd never been in prison before.' The prison staff were helpful and supportive, but Bob was deeply shaken by what had happened. 'I was feeling suicidal. I felt so lonely and so lost. My mum and dad are dead, and my wife and kids were all I had.' He had been at Horfield just over a month when a prison officer delivered a letter to his cell – a white, typed envelope sent by registered post. 'I didn't have a clue what it was.' On opening it, he discovered it was a solicitor's notification that his wife was proceeding with a divorce. 'I just broke down. I felt as if the whole world had been taken away from me.' It was decided that Bob should be housed in the prison's hospital wing and monitored. A doctor gave him what Bob calls 'knockout drops' – 'they calm you down but don't take away the feelings, the pain.'

Late that evening, Bob was alone in his cell – a room ten feet by eight feet, with a single bed, a table and chair, a sink and toilet, and a high barred window. It was after 'lock up' and the cell lights were out. Steel gates were banging as the prison officers moved round the jail and passed through the exercise yard outside. Guard dogs with officers on night patrol barked occasionally. 'There were no curtains and a great big floodlight outside, so my room was lit up. It must have been about midnight. I was lying there. I got up and took a bed sheet, tied it to the window bars and then around my neck. I stood on a chair…'

Bob was about to step off, when something happened. 'The room became very still and peaceful. I couldn't hear any other sounds. It was as though a warm flow went through me – I felt very calm. This was when I saw Jesus nailed to the cross – by the cell door. Initially, I was shocked. He was the full height of the room, real yet illuminated. It was a very bright light, but it didn't hurt your eyes. The cross was dark. You could see it behind him. It looked physical and real.' Bob then heard a voice speak to him. 'He said, "I forsook my son for your sins. There is no need to take your life. It doesn't matter what you've done or how alone you are – I love you and I want you."'

The experience lasted for around fifteen minutes.

Afterwards, Bob struggled for some time to undo the knotted sheets and get them back on to the bed. 'I was sitting there, and the flap in the door came up. The officer said, "Are you all right?" I said, "Yes". He said, "You look like you've seen a ghost!" I said, "Well ... maybe." I thought, *If I say anything now, they'll surely think I'm mad.*'

The next day Bob visited the prison chaplain and told him what he had seen. He said, 'Obviously someone is looking after you!' He suggested that Bob begin reading the Bible. 'I was still very tearful and weepy, but I felt a lot calmer in myself and I started going along to the chapel.' The 'knockout drops' were making him dopey and affecting his ability to read, so he asked to be taken off them. As his condition steadily improved, he was moved from the hospital wing to the main one.

After two weeks on the main wing, a prison officer informed him that he was being transferred to Rule 43, as there were whispers that Bob's life was at risk from assault by other inmates. 'Maybe someone had found out what my offence was.' This section of a prison houses inmates who need protection from other inmates, for whatever reason, including sex offenders, or 'nonces'. Those on Rule 43 are regarded with contempt by other prisoners. For their safety, they have different exercise and meal times, frequently needing to be personally escorted around the jail. Rule 43 prisoners would get 'all sorts' thrown at them from the cell windows above when they were in the yard. 'All sorts' could mean anything from glass fragments to personal waste.

During his time on this wing, Bob shared his cell with a Christian, Roy. Soon they started a group meeting for prayer and Bible reading. Bob was never hurt during his time here. 'We would pray and ask God to protect us, and we wouldn't get anything thrown at us. It seemed strange – other inmates would pass us by.' They saw further signs of God's love. 'One of the officers was a Christian, and he used to bring us in snacks and bits of cheese, do little favours for us.' Through Roy, Bob made a penfriend who wrote to him regularly. 'If I felt down, I would always get a letter of encouragement saying that God loved me and was always there for me.'

After two months at Horfield, Bob paid a special visit to the chaplain. 'I told him I wanted to confess my sins. I confessed them all and, once I'd done that, it was as though a big brick had been lifted right off me – I felt so relaxed and peaceful. I said to the chaplain, "I needed to do that."'

After attending classes, Bob was confirmed at a service conducted by the Bishop of Malmesbury in the prison chapel, allowing him from then on to receive Holy Communion. In August 1994, his case came before a court hearing. The police had dropped the charges of ABH: the offence was to be rape. 'As the barrister put it to me, although my wife had consented, she had done so out of fear. When I went into prison, I was going to plead not guilty. But I didn't want to put my wife through a full trial. I've done wrong, so I have to pay the price.' He pleaded guilty and was given a four-year sentence.

Bob left Horfield with a good report from the prison's senior officer. He believes that, by God's grace, he was allowed to serve most of his sentence at an open plan 'D' category prison, even though his offence meant he was a category 'C' prisoner. Bob eventually served two years and eight months in prison. His knowledge of God grew there and he feels that God helped him to cope. The chaplain put him in contact with a couple who visited and befriended him. If he was ever given home leave at Christmas, they said he could stay with them. 'To have people show affection and care for me was strange. From the first time I met them, the love I received really astounded me.'

On leaving jail in July 1996, Bob stayed in a single room in an ex-prisoners' halfway house in Bristol. He found a church, which he still belongs to. 'I felt part of a spiritual family. People there are interested in my welfare. The minister has helped me a lot. If I have a problem, I feel that I can talk to him.' Bob also found work driving lorries for an agency. The owner happened to be a Christian. 'We had a chat and I told him where I'd been. He said that it was no problem and that he was pleased to hear I was "one of the family"!'

With good references from the agency, he moved on to coach driving for National Express, working on the routes to London and the airports as well as Birmingham and Bradford. In March 1997, with the help of a couple from his church, who lent him the necessary deposit, he moved out of his single room and into his current home. After eighteen months with National Express, he took up his current coach-driving job. 'The boss told me it would be a month or so before I would be driving the big coaches. Within a fortnight I was driving them,' he says with amazement. 'God has had a hand in helping me to achieve what I have.'

Bob has found the love he'd been looking for all his life. This experience is epitomised by something that happened to him while he was still in prison. 'One Saturday morning, towards the end of my sentence, I was in my room when there was a knock on my door. I got out of bed to see who it was. But there was nobody on the landing. I closed the door and lay back down. Suddenly, the room went very peaceful and still. This lasted for about three or four minutes. It was as though someone put their arms around me and held me...'

Cherie

Chapter 3

CHERIE: THE LITTLE BLACK HANDGUN

When Cherie returned to the world of employment, she could never have anticipated the dramatic events that would drive her to despair. Seven years ago, having brought up her three children, she decided it was time to take a part-time job at a branch of a well-known high street building society a mile from the centre of Bristol. Cherie describes the office décor as 'a little drab', with wood panelling and a single counter running down the left-hand side past three cashier points.

Shortly after she started work, the branch was hit by two raids. 'Both robbers came in and pushed handwritten notes across the counter saying, "Fill this carrier bag. I've got a gun." During the first one, I was working at a nearby desk and wasn't actually aware of what had happened until it was all over. The cashier handed over maybe three hundred pounds. A note attached to a clip in the cash till activated the security camera, but she actually forgot to pull it out. I was a little shocked, but it didn't really worry me as I wasn't directly involved. We just supported each other, as no one had been hurt.' The police came and took statements, the building society played it down, and the women carried on working.

Not long after, a man wearing a crash helmet entered the branch. He stood looking uncomfortable at the information window close to where Cherie was serving. He was waiting for the banking hall to empty. 'I said, "Can I help you?" Moving round another customer, he came up and pulled out a gun. I remember him pointing it at me and saying, "Give me the money." It was a little black metal handgun, and I was looking down the end of it. It was so like something out of a movie that initially I thought it was a joke and said so. I backed away from him. He then grabbed the customer next to him, held the gun to his head and said, "I'm not joking." I gave him the money. I remember being really angry and swearing at him. I thought I hadn't given him that much, but when we checked the till later, it was about eight hundred pounds.'

The threatened customer followed the robber, walking at a discreet distance, all the way to his home. The police surrounded the house and he was caught. It transpired that he was just seventeen years old. 'He was robbing to get money for Christmas presents. It was just so ridiculous really, but it was scary.' It was also discovered that the gun was a replica.

This raid disturbed Cherie. 'At the time, I felt he would blame me for being caught. I was worried and frightened, that myself and the children might be in some kind of danger. I thought his friends might blame me or follow me. It was probably ridiculous, but I couldn't talk to anyone about it. It seemed like it had all got out of proportion in my head and was my problem rather than anyone else's.' The staff gave statements to the police and carried on working. The building society offered them some counselling in London, but London seemed like a long way to go.

Two more raids followed a couple of months later. Cherie recounts what was now the fifth robbery: 'I was sitting at a desk. I can remember looking up and seeing the cashier at the counter and this guy pointing a gun at her. It was a silver handgun with a barrel about six inches long. To me, it looked like a replica.' Her colleague handed over some money. The robber was again pursued round the back of the building society into some gardens, where he dumped his clothes and the gun in a bag. The police cordoned off the area, TV reporters arrived and the staff were confined to the premises for a difficult two-hour wait. This robber, too, was eventually caught. 'It transpired the gun was real and it was loaded. If he'd been frightened, you wonder what he'd have done. That made it particularly scary. He'd seen the previous robberies on *Crimestoppers* TV reconstructions and thought he'd have a go at it. He hadn't cottoned on that people who rob building societies often don't use real guns.'

The company expected the staff to keep the branch open, but this time they all refused to work for a couple of days.

Cherie was cooking the family tea one evening when she started to cry and couldn't stop. Again, counselling had been made available to the staff, but it hadn't really helped. 'I couldn't face anything – I was just so frightened all the time. I'd become afraid of everybody. I'd be walking down the street and, if someone pulled up in a car beside me just to ask for directions, I'd be scared. If someone tapped me on the shoulder, I'd hit the ceiling. I didn't want to go out, I didn't feel well and I couldn't control my emotions.'

Her doctor gave her antidepressants and referred her to a hospital psychiatrist. On a later visit to the same practice, which was staffed by Christians, a different doctor began to make regular time for her in his schedule, as she was repeatedly in a state of distress. 'Something obviously touched him – he felt he had to give me the time. He asked if I'd mind if he prayed for me. It is something I would have previously shied away from, as I would have said I was an atheist. But part of the reason I was prepared to listen to him was because he'd showed that he cared.' The doctor prayed for her and she came away feeling briefly calmer.

Post-traumatic stress disorder was the diagnosis of the hospital psychiatrist, who suggested she go back to work to help combat it. 'I went back for two weeks, but I just couldn't do it. It actually made me feel worse, because I seemed such a failure. I felt I'd lost a grip on my life – this was even more frightening and I wondered if I'd ever be normal again. I couldn't believe what was happening to me – I'd always been such a 'together' person. Now, I couldn't cope with my job. I couldn't cope with my three children. Everything was a struggle and I just couldn't break out of it. I began to feel I was going mad and that the person I had been was lost.'

Cherie took forty of her antidepressant tablets one Saturday evening before retiring for the night. 'My husband had already gone to bed. People say that attempted suicide is a cry for help, but I really didn't want to go on. I didn't think anyone could help me. My husband had tried to deal with it all in the best way he could, but it didn't help.' Later, as he slept beside her, one thought made her wake him in the early hours. She realised that he might get up in the morning and go to work, thinking she was asleep, and then the children would find her. In a state of disbelief, he tried to make her drink salt water and drove her quickly to the hospital. 'It was all a blur, really. They made me drink a big glass of charcoal water and put a tube into my stomach to wash it out. It was awful. After I'd recovered, I didn't feel any better. I was afraid I wouldn't ever get better.'

She discharged herself from hospital the next day. 'They wanted me to see a psychiatrist and be admitted as an in-patient, but I wouldn't. My sister-in-law had gone into a mental hospital and ultimately killed herself, so I wasn't going anywhere near them.' She agreed to visit a day centre at the hospital. 'It was just awful and I walked out in tears. They couldn't help me. That was the biggest thing – there was no one who could actually help me.'

A thought crossed her mind as she sat in her car in the hospital car park. 'I sat there and said – and I'm not proud of these words – "I've tried everything else, I'll try God." A feeling of peace and well-being immediately began to come over me. It was a physical warmth, and it actually continued for about six weeks. I felt wrapped in love. I just knew Jesus was there and he cared for me, and that made me feel better. I know it sounds very simplistic, but that's how it was. To express it, all words seem inadequate.'

She drove to see the manager of the practice where her doctor worked – a Christian who she knew would talk with her – and began to meet with her regularly. 'I felt as though God had wrapped a blanket round me. I just felt unbelievably better. It was as if by saying, "I will try God", everything changed – I'd opened the door. It was absolutely dynamic. I went home and my husband couldn't believe the change in me. I never took another antidepressant. I never looked back. My sister says to me, "Oh, you found an inner strength, blah-di-blah", but I just know that isn't how it was.'

Cherie's doctor later told her she had made an unprecedented recovery. 'I felt that if Jesus loved me, I could look in the mirror and love myself. I was healed of my fear of everything and everybody – a huge thing to be carrying around. But Jesus says that it's his peace which drives away fear.'

When Cherie returned to work one month later, the office had been refurbished with bullet-proof steel screens. 'If someone threatened us, we were to press a button and the screen would shoot up in a third of a second.' Working life continued without incident for a number of months, and Cherie was promoted to assistant branch manager. But, as if on cue in some malevolent cycle, two more raids occurred. 'At the end of November, the first guy came in wearing a woolly hat pulled down. He pointed a gun at the cashier, she shot the screen up and he ran off. A week to the day later, two lads came in and one of them jumped the counter. He put his foot up and was just straight over. The cashier still had to fire up the screen on building society instructions, so he was trapped in the back with us, panicking and running around. Meanwhile, his accomplice was out in the banking hall, denting the screen and smashing the perspex office windows with a scaffolding pole. The manager opened one of the cash trays and gave the trapped robber some money, and I let him out.' The robbers fled.

Cherie's post-traumatic stress symptoms began to return. She went back to talk to her doctor. He said, 'You've got to decide between your health and a career, because you're not going to cope with this indefinitely.' The building society made the decision to close the branch down anyway, and Cherie and the branch manager decided to leave and take redundancy.

The robberies had disturbed other staff at the branch. 'I was the one who seemed to be most affected by the raids at the time. But, over the years, I've kept in touch with three of the ladies involved and they are all still affected by it. One of them, a young girl present at the last two raids, struggled for ages and was off sick. She took redundancy and went to work somewhere where she wouldn't be in contact with the public. It was eighteen months after the branch closed before she found a sympathetic GP. One of the other ladies says she still has dreams about it. They are still living with it all six years on.

'I needed somewhere quiet and safe to work, with people who understood what had happened to me.' The doctors' surgery where she was a patient had a vacancy for a receptionist, which fitted the bill, and she got it. 'I think it would have been quite difficult getting another job at that stage, with my history. It could have been a different story if they hadn't had the faith in me to give me a job. It gave me a chance to get my confidence back.'

Two years ago, Cherie moved to a new job managing the 'on call' hours of a cooperative of sixty-two doctors. 'When I think about what I took on, I surprised myself. But I just felt ready for a challenge. I really enjoy the job I do now. It has given me the chance to extend my skills considerably and I feel fulfilled. Everybody comments on what a good team spirit there is; people seem to be happy working there. I think some of this reflects what I have tried to put in: I always try to treat colleagues the way God would want me to.'

Cherie is confident about the lasting importance of her car park encounter. 'I'm seven years down the line and I still feel that Jesus is there and part of my life. Once you become a Christian, read the Bible and accept the way God wants you to live, it does change your life. When I'm faced with decisions, I'm always asking myself what God would want me to do. Sometimes it's hard, but I do feel that if I live my life on that basis, I'm blessed because of it. I'm just a different person now.'

Robin

Chapter 4

ROBIN: AN ALTERED STATE OF MIND

Pop festival crowds gather by an outdoor stage set up at the bottom of the valley. On a hill overlooking the stage, a circular encampment huddles up to the skyline. Large military-green tents, buses with billowing awnings attached and a tepee fit for a chief surround the smoking white ashes of a wood fire. Small groups of people sit around on groundsheets or neatly arranged logs, quietly singing. Others squat with their eyes closed in silent reflection or raise their hands upward in supplication. A lone dog lopes through, oblivious to it all.

An untethered tent flap flips wildly in the wind. Robin picks up a mallet and secures it with a metal tent-peg of circus proportions. 'We are a good team together and I have become part of it,' he says. 'I'm one of the site crew. I like to help organise the tents, and load and unload the bus. People come into the circle of Lighting Fires and quickly feel at home. We are a growing family.'

Robin only recently started helping the Lighting Fires community at the festivals they visit. His association with festival-goers, however, began in the early 1980s. 'I lived in a very suburban area of Hampshire, Chandlers Ford, which was quite a boring place to live as a teenager. The only thing to do was to go to the pub and drink. I got in with a crowd of people who would sit in the corner with inane grins, and I started smoking cannabis and taking magic mushrooms. I found it suited my imagination more than getting depressed on alcohol.' One evening he was caught smoking at the back of the pub by the police. He was nineteen and had never been in trouble with them before. He told the truth, and got himself into bigger trouble by grassing the dealer up. Robin was then socially ostracised.

He now found himself looking for a new crowd. 'I was a punk at the time, so I went down to a pub in Southampton, which had a bit of a punk scene. I began hanging around there with the people I got chatting to while playing pool or being zonked out. I was very unhappy and dissatisfied at the time. I'd had a job for a couple of years in the drawing office of Southampton University, drawing maps mainly for the geography department. It was a good job, but the atmosphere in the office was a bit dead. There wasn't anything that was fulfilling me. I'd let drop a lot of my active social life, like skateboarding and canoeing.'

The Derby Road area in Southampton was well known for being a red-light district. One evening, on a bus, he met a friend of his brother's, who invited him along to a wine bar there. 'The place was like a supermarket for drugs, and it became a lot worse in the years I frequented it. It was full of people who would go to Stonehenge and other festivals, and some parts of the bar were managed by the Hell's Angels. So it was quite a heavy scene. But it became my home from home for the next five years.'

He became friendly with a couple of punks who rented a nearby flat. They invited him round and he became their live-in friend for the next two years. 'I started to take speed and trip on acid a lot. I would occasionally do cocaine,

Valium, uppers, downers, DF118s and any other medical drugs that were around. As time went on, I looked for other drugs. They offered a form of excitement, alleviated the boredom, and helped me to cope, I suppose. It was a compensation for something, but I don't know that it did my mind a lot of good. I spent a lot of time with my own thoughts. The drugs put me in a big bubble, really.'

Robin's thoughts began to turn increasingly towards searching questions about life. 'I began to think about this big university I was working in, and how all its science didn't seem to have the answers to some of the issues I could see happening in the world, like green issues and how mankind was chewing up the earth. Even though I was surrounded by all this brain power, it seemed to be part of the problem. Something in me said there has got to be a better answer than science and progress.'

During a growing number of tea-break chats, a new girl in the drawing office introduced Robin to what he calls 'the Sixties' thing'. 'She brought a spiritual dimension to my life. I started getting interested in Zen and what God was. I read *Zen and The Art of Motorcycle Maintenance*, science fiction books and Franz Kafka. I was looking for reading that would complete this search going on inside me. My brother got me interested in skateboarding again and that had spiritual overtones – to do it well, you had to be into the Tao of skateboarding. To balance and perform good tricks, your mind and body had to be in harmony.'

By the late eighties Robin had cut back on the heavier drugs, but he was still smoking cannabis. One particular incident remains with him, when he was visiting friends one afternoon. 'One of them gave me this joint, which I smoked, and it did something to my head that didn't agree with me. I can still remember it quite vividly. I felt it affect my brain in a very adverse manner. Some sort of depression or oppression came over me, and I remember going home in a bit more of a bubble that afternoon.'

Round about this time, he began to experience a new sense of wonder at the natural world, especially birds. 'I felt there was something good in nature talking to me.' Birds, notably robins, were speaking to him in very specific ways about his drug use, telling him he should stop. Whether it was down to feathered agents of the divine, or chemicals and his imagination, change was certainly about to happen. In the autumn of 1988 he was accepted on a BTEC Art and Design course at a college in Bath, and moved to live in the city. Once on the course, however, he felt that some of the students didn't accept him and that there were other people in the city who 'had it in for him'. He also believed that people were putting drugs in his food. 'I suppose I got a bit paranoid.'

He was skateboarding in one of the city's parks when he learned of a ramp in the garden of a central vicarage. The minister had built it for his sons, but it was available for others to use. As he practised his skateboarding tricks there, he found the minister and his wife friendly and ready to listen. 'One particular afternoon, instead of going to skateboard, I went saying that I needed some help. They asked me if I would like to be prayed for, so we went into the minister's study. There were three other people besides me – the minister, his wife and one of their friends – but I knew there was someone else, too. I couldn't quite see him, but I was aware of a spiritual presence. Though I didn't think of it at the time, I know now that it was Jesus.'

He visited the vicarage over the next couple of weeks for further conversations. On one occasion, he said a prayer to confess some of the things he'd done wrong, and asked Jesus to help him turn his life around. 'I knew I'd come into contact with something that was going to be an answer, that was going to be fulfilling and of great comfort to me. I remember walking up to the vicarage one particular morning, when a robin crossed my path. I looked at the hills on the opposite side of the city and I realised that the whole of creation was alive with God. I was invited to church one morning and it was like coming home. I sat on the back row, among all these friendly faces. Before I'd had friends and acquaintances, but not people who I felt at home with and comfortable about.'

Robin began attending the church. 'I felt there was a tangible presence in the worship services. This was when I knew that God had come to earth and that he empathised with us so much, he was willing to die and take away our sins.' He completed his arts foundation course and then went on to take A level ceramics. He was shortly to give up using illegal substances completely, but he had not yet done so. 'Because I'd taken drugs for quite a long time, I had a lot of their residues in my mind. I could feel all this stuff going round in my brain. I used to say, "Come on, Lord. I'm really sorry I've done all this stuff. I don't want it there any more. Heal me!" ' The flashbacks from the drugs diminished and, after about eighteen months, he found that his thoughts were a lot more lucid. 'I could write my essays for college a lot better than I had before, and I could concentrate more. It was as if the Holy Spirit was cleaning my brain out. I felt like I wasn't going round so much, or up so high, on the acid residues left in there.'

One evening, a visiting speaker to the church asked for a 'minor miracle', praying with his hand over Robin's head. 'As I walked home, I felt the capacity of my brain being returned to me. I could feel Jesus physically healing me. Afterwards, as I was walking along, thinking about things, I could feel my mind popping back into place. It happened two or three times on that walk home. It was quite an amazing experience.'

Further incidents left a deep impression on him. On returning from the WOMAD festival in 1989, he visited a local house-church near his parent's home, where an evangelist was speaking. He asked if people wanted to come forward for prayer, and Robin's hand went up. 'He prayed that the Holy Spirit would work in my life, and I was filled with this light too powerful to stand up to. I thought, *I can stand up to this – I won't fall down*, but I found that I just couldn't stay upright. This was when I knew that he was utterly invincible, utterly omnipotent, that he really was this almighty, powerful God, just full of so much light.'

Alone at the church in Bath, Robin made a commitment at the altar to follow Jesus as Lord. 'There wasn't any great answer. I said, "I don't know what you've got for me next. I'll do these few things that I can, as far as getting into pottery is concerned." ' After completing his A level ceramics course, he went on, in the early nineties, to pass an HND in ceramics in Derby, where he now lives. He has since studied calligraphy and recently obtained a grade A in A level photography. 'I feel that God began to redeem the works of my hands by giving me these creative courses to go on. I definitely feel led to be a potter. And hopefully, with the kiln I now have, I'll get a workshop and manage to start making pots. I feel that God has gifted me to make pots...'

Robin no longer uses any mind-altering substances. 'I used to be fearful of people around me, like I was being watched. I felt uneasy and that I had nowhere to turn. But now I do have somewhere to turn, because God is my Father and shield. I don't have to be watching my back any more, or worry that others have got it in for me.'

He made contact with the organiser of a group of travelling Christians – Lighting Fires, as it later became known – at the Glastonbury music festival in 1992. The group regularly set up their encampments at music festivals like Glastonbury and Phoenix, and have visited other gatherings on the Isle of Skye and at pagan outposts and stone circles. 'I found that they were very like-minded and from a 'crusty' background, and I wanted to stay involved with alternative people and travellers, having come from such a background myself. They are the people I feel most comfortable with.' The group meet together for Christian worship and prayer, and to welcome others into their midst. 'A lot of people from alternative scenes say they feel at home with us, because of our tents and the way we build our community at a festival. We accept people as they come, no matter how broken they are.'

With amusing irony, Robin recounts one incident about some of the first Christians he met, whose beliefs he would later come to share. 'I remember meeting two girls on a train to Farnborough. There was something about them, and I wanted to know what they were on. I could perceive something very good about them. I thought it was chemically induced...'

Ernesto

Chapter 5

ERNESTO: TIME AND MOTION

Like much of Latin America, Peru was a turbulent and dangerous place to live back in the mid-eighties. A civil conflict was raging in the country between the rural Shining Path and urban Tupac Amaru guerrilla groups, and the government's security forces and covert paramilitary units. The guerrillas' bombing campaigns were beginning to strike seemingly indiscriminate civilian targets in the capital, Lima. At that time, Ernesto was a student of anthropology at the city's San Marcos University, and took part in demonstrations in an environment of widespread poverty and repression. The university was seen as a centre of Marxist activity, but Ernesto was not a Marxist: he was a Christian. 'Some people who studied with me took the Shining Path option. I never believed in the armed route, but I believed in social justice. The political situation had reached a very critical point in Peru – things had started to become heavy, particularly in my university. My mother was very concerned about my safety. I think she felt that every time she said goodbye, she did not know if she would see me again.'

For his own and his family's peace of mind, he decided to visit a friend in Brazil for a month until the tensions eased. It was the January of 1987. 'I didn't want to leave. I left Peru once before, in 1980, but it didn't work out. It was an awful experience, so I said to myself, "Never again." This time round it seemed as though circumstances were pushing me out, but it was actually something else. It would be wrong to say that we are just passive entities in the universe and God plays chess with us. There is a mystery in all this. Despite our desire to do things, it is as if there were something there behind the scenes operating a master plan. At that point, I didn't think such thoughts. To me, it just seemed that the future was bleak and I didn't know what would happen to me.'

The military cracked down on the university shortly after Ernesto arrived in Saõ Paulo – he learnt about events in a letter from his mother. 'One night they broke into the campus, went to the accommodation area and took everybody. Two girls, who were friends of the family, were taken by the police but released later. That wasn't the case for everybody, however...'

Ernesto could not return to Peru. With the university closed, he felt there was no longer a forum for free expression in his country. And how could he study? 'I remember one afternoon – I was on my own and I broke down. I cried for hours and I didn't know why. It was as if I were releasing the pain from inside me. The question kept popping into my mind: What am I doing here?'

Ernesto had only a small amount of savings, but his friend let him stay free of charge for the time being. 'I thought originally I would stay in Brazil. But if you are a Brazilian living in your own country, whatever happens you have your family around you to support and protect you. I was a foreigner; I didn't have anybody.'

He began to consider using his remaining money to go to Spain: there at least they spoke Spanish and life would seem a little less foreign! Through a business speculation with a friend, however, Ernesto lost all of his money. The same friend helped him get a small design job which paid him more than he'd lost, but caused him to delay travel until the May of that year. 'It worked out very well. This has been the pattern throughout my life. Always, God's timing is the right time. Things happen when they have to happen and you only realise it later. Things didn't happen in March, when I really wanted to go. But it was just as well, as I had left Peru with only a light denim jacket and didn't have the money to buy warm clothes for the winter weather of Spain. It was one small, practical example of God's timing for me.'

Just before he left Saõ Paulo, a conversation with a girl-friend made a lasting impression on him. 'She was a very spiritually aware Christian. She said to me, "What is coming in your life is going to be very tough. I am going to pray for you. But when you go through these things, you will see what Jesus will do for you." I never thought that what was coming would be tough. If I had considered it, I would have probably chickened out.'

With just 5,000 pesetas in his pocket, Ernesto flew into the mild May weather of Madrid. His only contact was a friend he had met travelling seven years earlier, who now lived in Barcelona. Using 3,000 pesetas, he took the coach directly there. His friend was happy to put him up, but only for a week. However, as a consequence, he began attending a church in the city and was given the help he needed over the six months he was to remain in Spain. An American missionary offered him a place to sleep for a couple of weeks. Another member of the church gave him a bed in return for more design work. A Colombian couple gave him money to rent a flat. In return, he did little jobs for the church. 'People really adopted me, especially one guy who was like a brother to me. He took me under his wing, and I spent a lot of time at his house. The church came to see me not simply as a victim, but as someone who could make a contribution.' When Ernesto could no longer pay his bills, the pastor invited him to live in his house. 'At that time they had four kids and were living in a flat. They took me in for three months, fed me and treated me as a part of the family. I have never experienced so much love.'

Ernesto's sister had emigrated to Europe a couple of years earlier. As Christmas approached, she invited him to stay with her in England. Ernesto could not afford to make the trip and, to complicate matters, he had lost his passport. Getting a new one from the Peruvian embassy could take months! But, shortly afterwards, he was offered a job decorating a flat, and was given 20,000 pesetas on completing it. It was just enough to buy a plane ticket. 'I hadn't had any work paid like that before. Two days after I had finished, I rang the embassy and they said they had received quick authorisation. I was paid, I collected my passport and bought the ticket. God's timing was as evident in Spain as it had been in Brazil.'

His sister met him at a wet Gatwick Airport at the end of November 1987. After spending a few weeks with her, he began, on her suggestion, to learn English and to think about remaining in the UK a little longer. 'I didn't want to stay here. I didn't like the weather. I didn't like England. The church had been very important for me in Spain. Not just because of the people, but somehow I made a lot of peace with my faith. One thing I never understood in Peru was what Jesus had meant when he said, "If you follow me and leave your parents and brothers and sisters, you will have more mothers, fathers and brothers." In Spain I really knew what he meant – many of the people there became my mothers, my fathers, my brothers, as I never have experienced before in my life.' In England, however, he felt bereft of that family warmth.

Nevertheless, Ernesto decided to renew his visa as a student and develop a childhood talent, building up his art portfolio. After two years living with his sister, he moved to Oxford, where he met a Chilean working with refugees in the city. They became friends and organised art exhibitions together. 'He wanted to know more about me. At that time I was very reluctant to tell people my story. I did not want to be perceived as a victim.' Ernesto, nevertheless, explained his circumstances to his friend, who told him, 'You have enough reasons to fear for your life if you go back to Peru. Have you considered applying for political asylum?'

'I didn't know anything about this. He said that if I did, I wouldn't be able to return to my country until the situation there had changed.' Ernesto thought about it and reluctantly decided to go ahead. He knew it would mean he could not leave the UK until the process was complete. It was one of the grimmest days of his life – he felt like he was putting himself in a jail.

With the help of an asylum charity, Ernesto presented his case. It took three years before he was actually called for his interview. Then, after hours of interviewing, they rejected his story. 'They said that they didn't believe the things I said, or that I was in danger. If you don't have marks on your body where you have been tortured, it is very hard to get them to acknowledge your story.' A year later, Ernesto was served with a deportation order. He appealed against it, and was notified that his case would be considered the following Christmas by an independent adjudicator. This was now 1996.

One of the grounds for the Home Office's rejection of his case concerned a meeting Ernesto had had with the Liberal Democrat MP, Simon Hughes, to discuss the human rights situation in Peru. During his interview for asylum, Ernesto, questioned about any contact with political parties in the UK, had told them about this sole dinner engagement. Odd as it may seem, they thought it unlikely he had met the MP and that, by extension, he was lying about other matters. When Simon Hughes simply wrote a letter to corroborate that they had indeed met, the case was withdrawn before it went to adjudication. In October 1998, two years later, after seven years of waiting, he was finally sent a letter granting him permanent leave to remain in the UK.

While the uncertainties of the asylum process were taking their course, Ernesto's art was flowering as never before. This is something he feels God gave back to him here. He turned from occasional commercial illustration to painting, and began exhibiting his work widely. In 1997, he initiated the opening of the Ark T gallery in Oxford, where he now exhibits the work of painters and photographers from the UK and around the world. But the break-up of a relationship, and a sudden, traumatic asthma attack while he waited to hear from the Home Office, pushed him into a trough of despair. 'I had a really deep, existential crisis. There was a big hole in my life. I'd reached a point where I thought there was no God, and felt a deep sense of emptiness and loneliness.' Reflecting on this, he compares himself to the people of Israel who, despite having seen the amazing miracles of God as they were led out of Egypt, still forgot about them and complained. 'These experiences gave me a level of understanding of the human condition: your pain is *your* pain; you can be surrounded by people who love you, but there is nothing they can do for you. In other words, you are alone. Existential pain is something most people face sooner or later. It pushed me to the realisation that, without God, there is nothing there – it is a cold, dark, empty world. Maybe this is the reason why many artists commit suicide: they are so spiritually and emotionally aware, so engaged in searching for something – and often they don't find it. Without God, the universe is an empty space, and emptiness is the most terrible feeling you can have.'

Ernesto felt that life was becoming just too difficult. Overwhelmed, he turned to his Bible for the first time in a long while. 'I opened it up and I said, "Jesus, if you are there, you have to speak to me now – because if you don't, and in a direct way, I'm going to end this existence." ' Then he opened the Bible three times, each time reading a specific passage which seemed to make striking sense to him. Jesus spoke to him by making connections with his past. One passage he read was about 'wisdom'. As a teenager, Ernesto had wanted to be like the Old Testament king, Solomon – wise in matters of human experience. 'Wisdom had been an issue for me since I was a kid. I thought, *This an extremely amazing coincidence*. It was as though Jesus was saying, "You have tried to be wise, but you have been foolish. The only real wisdom is that which comes from me. What went wrong was that you tried to pursue your own wisdom. And look at the state of your life now." '

A week later, Ernesto had a further powerful experience as he lay in bed at his sister's house. He felt the Holy Spirit flow over him like an energy, and it brought to mind people he needed to forgive. 'I was crying a lot. When I woke up the following morning, the pain was still there, but I felt as if a heaviness had been lifted. It reminded me that Jesus' love was there to forgive me, too.' After this, over the next few weeks, Ernesto saw deeper healing in his life. 'There are different kinds of healing, but probably the healing that everybody needs is the one that makes sense of their own experience. My life felt like fragmented pieces, without connections. But, after my encounter with the Holy Spirit, I started to see my whole life with new eyes. Everything was making sense and had a place. This was when I began to appreciate God's timing. It is only as time passes that you see how God has worked in your life. Then, from that perspective, looking back, you can see the landscape, the shape of your past. I don't think you can enjoy your present if you don't have peace with your past.'

Despite all the uncertainty he has encountered, God's presence has clearly left Ernesto richer. 'I think the fact that I've had to leave my country, my family, my friends and my roots has helped me to realise how much we base our lives on the securities we build. We don't know where we are going and we don't have control over it. So much advertising on TV is about being in control of your life, your money, your future, in order to have peace of mind. The Christian message is the opposite: give up control to Jesus and then you will have peace of mind. So much of what I have gone through in life has taught me this. Maybe if I had stayed in my country, I would never have realised it.'

Catherine

Chapter 6

CATHERINE: WILL SHE GO TO THE BALL?

A large, central double bed dominates the room at Catherine's parents' house on a leafy avenue in Swindon. She regards it reflectively as she sits on the settee. She has spent many long months there.

Six years ago, shortly after her twentieth birthday, Catherine came down with a spate of throat infections and flu-like symptoms. Eventually she took what she thought would be a few days off, but, within the space of a few weeks, it became apparent that she wasn't going to recover. She had tests for glandular fever and other illnesses, but they all came back negative.

'It was quite shocking,' she tells me. Over four weeks, in September 1993, her health continued to decline. By the middle of the month she was virtually housebound. 'I had sharp stabbing pains and every joint and muscle was aching. I couldn't cope with loud noises or more than one sound at the same time. My body temperature was in extremes of hot and cold. The fatigue was so bad, just walking around the house was exhausting. Even brushing my hair was hard.' Catherine was never able to return to her study placement as a student nurse. A consultant at Princess Margaret Hospital in Swindon diagnosed her as suffering from chronic fatigue syndrome: ME.

Her condition did not improve for the next two years

and she remained confined to the home. Though she was still able to do basic self-help tasks, her husband was looking after everything else. 'He coped very well with the illness, but the marriage was going from bad to worse. I took a lot out on him – my frustration at being unhappy in the marriage anyway, plus I found out he was having an affair. It was a case of both sides being at fault, and a bad situation just exploded.' She moved back to her parents' home to be cared for there. 'Although I wasn't in love with my husband, suddenly my world had fallen apart. It was really tough.'

Catherine's relationship with her parents during her teenage years had been very difficult. They were practising Christians and, though she had attended church as a child, she later stopped going. 'I decided early on in the illness that I was going to make it without God. I was going to show my family that you didn't need God to get over something.' One of her sisters offered to pray for her, however. At first Catherine declined the offer, but later she consented. At that point she felt a huge weight lift off her, and then a deep feeling of peace.

A group of Christians meeting at her parents' home began to pray with her for her healing. Shortly after this, she made a personal commitment to Jesus as the Son of God. The prayer for healing continued through the summer of 1995, when she began to get a little better. 'I was convinced that Jesus was beginning a healing process in me, which made me feel I could begin a part-time course in psychology.' With her parents taking care of her, she coped with the study by doing little else and resting afterwards. However, by the following January, her condition deteriorated again and she was able to do less and less.

Catherine was taken to visit Holy Trinity on Old

Brompton Road in London, a church with a reputation for being alive with the work of the Holy Spirit. Here, she believes, God spoke to her with a message of encouragement given by a member of the congregation, that 'she would have more time in her chrysalis before she emerged as a butterfly'. 'I can remember being strongly impacted by it. Something big happened for me spiritually. I really came alive.'

Physically, she declined more and more, despite this spiritual encouragement. Yet she had a growing sense that Jesus was going to bring healing. But this would need to be preceded by healing in her relationships with her parents. 'There was a lot of hurt, and nothing had ever been acknowledged or dealt with. Things had been swept under the carpet.'

By June 1996, Catherine was completely bed-bound. Her mother gave up work to look after her. 'I fought it like mad, but it just got to the stage where I couldn't any more. Physically, it was horrendous. I had to be washed and fed, and take a wheelchair to the toilet. Cognitive stimulation – TV, reading, music, even conversation – was exhausting. The bedroom door had to be closed because I found noises in the house just too much. People would come and visit me, then just sit because they couldn't talk to me or do anything.' Despite this, on a spiritual level, Catherine was soaring. She had a deep sense of peace and joy, a confidence that God was in control.

A place was found for her in a specialist ME unit at a hospital in Romford. In the September she was moved there in an ambulance, to be placed under the care of a team. The programme aimed to find a basic level of activity with which a ME sufferer could cope without relapsing, then build on it. 'They started me off feeding myself three spoonfuls of food three times a day, reading five words twice a day, having two slots of fifteen minutes for conversation.' Catherine made relatively good progress, increasing these activities steadily. After six weeks, she left the hospital to continue the programme at home. 'I was very encouraged. I really believed Jesus was going to heal me through this programme, and that it would be at an accelerated rate. My sister was getting married the following August, and I was determined I was going to be at the wedding as the chief bridesmaid.'

Six weeks later, Catherine pushed herself beyond her limits and relapsed. 'I was as bad as I had been in the summer, if not worse. The family was absolutely gutted, and I felt as though a dark cloud had come over me. I fell into a lot of self-condemnation and guilt. I thought, *Why should Jesus intervene and get me to the wedding? It was all my fault.* I can remember exclaiming in January, "Oh, I will still be stuck at home like Cinderella!" ' Catherine was back at square one on the programme.

She took Holy Communion with her mother round about this time. They had drawn closer and were able to talk about the difficulties that existed in their relationship. 'We were grabbing all the time we could, to talk through issues and pray about the past. It was wonderful.'

In February 1997, another clear message of encouragement was given to Catherine through a friend from church, who had been praying for her. He brought it to her in her room. The specific words were that 'she would go to the ball'. Catherine knew straight away that it referred to the wedding. She couldn't wait to tell her mother. However, her mother had also sensed the Holy Spirit speaking to her about her daughter's healing. 'She had seen the caption, "You shall go to the ball", in a shop window, but she was too frightened to believe it was a word God was giving her for me.' Catherine felt this was indeed a firm promise from Jesus that she would be healed. She and her mum were on cloud nine. One week later she was given a picture drawn by the same friend's five-year-old daughter. The child was aware that Catherine was ill, but unaware of her father's message of encouragement. The picture was of a butterfly and a speech bubble containing the words, 'You will go to the ball'. Catherine held on to the hope it gave her.

Catherine's relationship difficulties with her father were also being addressed. 'Between February and Easter, God did an amazing work between my parents and me.' On Easter day, she felt God was saying to her that everything which had needed to happen before her healing could take place was now complete. 'I was in my bed as usual and the sunlight was pouring in. I was soaking in the sun and God's presence, when I heard him say in a still, small voice inside me, "It is finished. It is finished." '

After Easter, 'it was a roller-coaster ride. There were times when I thought I was going to be healed at such and such a time. I'd go through a countdown and get all my hopes up, and then it wouldn't happen. I'd have to pick up and carry on. But I kept hanging on to the promise. In my mind I thought God would heal me way before the wedding, because there was so much to prepare.'

After further prayer, Catherine sensed that she should 'walk out' her healing. She began to work through her programme at an accelerated rate and made good progress. One day she decided to tackle the stairs, even though she felt that God was warning her against this. But she went ahead – and relapsed. 'It was more severe than ever before. I couldn't even sit up to be fed. It was horrendous. Everybody went into a state of despair.'

Doubts were now being raised about Catherine's hopes for healing. Her sister Erica and Erica's fiancé Scott desperately wanted her to be at their wedding, but were concerned. 'My father, who was also my doctor, had by this time become quite knowledgeable about ME and was already becoming known as a specialist in the area. He knew that, for my degree of severity, you're talking five to ten years before you reach any basic quality of life.'

Nevertheless, five different people, independently, were sure God had confirmed to them that Catherine would be healed. A little over a month before the wedding, in mid-July, a group from her church started meeting to pray regularly for her, as this was their feeling about the situation, too. 'At one point I was getting worse still, but I was holding on to the promise.'

She went ahead in faith and had her bridesmaid's dress made. The measurements were loosely taken by her mother while she lay in bed. However, a week before her sister's wedding her condition had not improved. 'All these months I'd been lying in bed, thinking Jesus would heal me way before this. Surely there would be a huge bright light, or I'd get zapped, or just something big.'

With three days to go, a friend came to say that God had confirmed to her that it would happen. The friend wished God had picked on someone else to give her this message, because of the responsibility of what she was saying. But she felt that Catherine was now to 'walk out' into her healing. That same day Catherine began to test it out. 'The dressmaker came, and I stood for five minutes while she fitted it. I was in excruciating pain. Everything in my head was saying, "You are going to relapse", but I was standing. At that time, taking a couple of steps would have caused a relapse.' The rest of the day, she began to steadily break her routine.

The next day, Catherine continued to push against her condition. She began by sitting up in bed and walking to the bathroom. 'People seemed to be coming and going all day, and I was talking non-stop. The pain and fatigue kept coming, but the more I pushed through, the more they receded. Each step was a step of faith. It was like walking out over an abyss on an invisible bridge. By the end of the day I'd given myself a shower – I hadn't done that for sixteen months. It was incredible! On the Saturday I carried on where I'd left off. I arranged for a hairdresser to come and cut and blow-dry my hair. It was just absolutely amazing. I knew it was Jesus.'

That evening she decided to try the stairs– she couldn't wait any longer. 'My sister was with me. I got down about three steps and I began to panic. It felt like it was too much. Erica said to me, "No, Cath, keep going." By the time I got downstairs, I felt like I could have gone on forever. I crept into the kitchen and I said, "Hi, Mum." Her face was just a picture.'

On the day of her sister's wedding, 24 August 1997, people were rushing round the house, with hair being done in one room and make-up in another. 'I just got on with it. I went early to the church with my other sister, Rosie, so that people would see me before Erica came and it wouldn't detract from her. There was a huge ripple. All the time I was feeling the fatigue and pain, but I kept pushing through. Then Erica entered the church, and I followed her and my dad down the aisle. It was an amazing time. The service was wonderful. I stood for all the photos. We drove off to a beautiful manor, and I cried because it was so beautiful. I ate what I liked at the reception for the first time in four years. I had a bit to drink. I danced in the evening. I was one of the last to leave at midnight. I'd lasted about seventeen hours.'

Catherine was still in a dream the next day, when she continued to feel normal and healthy. She couldn't believe it. 'The day after that, my legs seized up so much, I couldn't get out of bed – my muscles hadn't done anything for so long. A friend of my dad's, who used to be a gym instructor in the Army, gave me some excruciating massages. He used an electric sander covered with a towel to finish off. That freed my legs up.'

After steadily building up her strength over the following months, in November Catherine left for a ten-day holiday in the Dominican Republic. She was deeply grateful to God. 'It was an amazing time. I felt that I was taken to a new level, physically. I swam and snorkelled in the Atlantic. I played tennis and went horse riding. At the beginning of December, I had a check-up at the Social Security's medical centre. I said, "Look! I'm healed! I'm healed!" She tested my muscles and couldn't believe the strength...'

Sarah

Chapter 7

SARAH: VOICES OF DARKNESS

The decision for Sarah as to whether or not she should use her real name in this account was something she thought over hard. How would family members unaware of her past react on reading it? Would certain persons featured in this story still attempt to exert some dark influence over her should they too discover it? These considerations were, however, not the most significant. Sarah is still conscious of a particular vulnerability which came from having felt personally invaded as the events recounted here unfolded in her life. She now wishes to protect herself from a different type of exposure. Because of this, the names of places and people have been changed. The photo, however, is of Sarah.

Sarah rented a small terrace house close to her parents' home in the West Yorkshire town of Wakefield. She had returned to her home town after graduating from Cardiff University in the late eighties, and had started to work at writing a radio play and short stories about South Wales life. 'I felt quite lonely at the time,' she recalls. 'A lot of the friends I'd known had moved away. Like everybody, I craved intimacy and was considering the possibility of finding a boyfriend.'

Then something peculiar happened to her. She found herself attracted to someone in a way she hadn't felt since she was a sixteen-year-old schoolgirl. 'I saw this bloke from a distance while I was writing in the college library, and I began to get really obsessed with him. He had all the signs of being a person who would be interested in the same things as me, and I got this strange feeling he was attracted to me, too. It's to do with body language, I suppose.'

She spotted him again at an animal rights event in the Students Union building and invented an excuse to talk. 'It was almost like he was just waiting for this, and he kind of dragged me off to the coffee bar. Immediately, it was as if we already knew each other.' Things developed quickly. They began meeting up in the library, and Sarah would invite him back to her house for tea. His name was Mitch. 'In a way, I found it all very exciting. But, in another way, I thought, *I don't really like this*.'

Sarah discovered that Mitch was sharing a room with his girlfriend, but it looked as if the relationship was going to end. 'Even though I had some morals, I thought, *Well, this relationship is on its last legs – it's obvious he doesn't want to be involved in it. It wouldn't be such a crime if we did get together*. But everything was just so boundary-less.' She also perceived something else that was odd. 'When I sat next to him, I sensed a real blackness – I can only describe it as blackness – a real darkness and bleakness inside him.' There had been a lot of suffering in his family, and Sarah put it down to this. Gradually, she noticed that Mitch was very charismatic and that a lot of people were attracted to him. He seemed to be someone who made things happen.

She was due to attend her degree ceremony in Cardiff that Easter. When Mitch invited her to visit him at his mother's house nearby, she accepted. 'His girlfriend actually asked me what I was doing at Easter. I told her I was going down to my graduation ceremony. She said, "Oh, where's that?" "Cardiff," I said. She looked at me and I knew that she knew what was going on. But nothing was said. Then we were laughing about something else when, all of a sudden, she changed. She became very serious and said, "I wouldn't mess with me if I were you. I know someone who can put curses on people." It was such an extraordinary thing to say, because she didn't appear to be involved in the occult or anything. She just seemed a perfectly normal person. I put it to one side, as I didn't have any kind of framework in which to accommodate this kind of thing.'

After the ceremony, Sarah went ahead and met up with Mitch. On their first night together, they drove along country lanes to an old pub. Mitch's driving was totally anarchic. 'On the way back he drove so crazily that his friend, who had come along with us, was screaming for him to stop. I just didn't know what was going on.' Later that evening they told each other how they felt. 'Against my better judgement, I decided to sleep in his bed with him – but we didn't have sex. It was really weird. I started getting palpitations and it wasn't pleasant. I began to feel quite scared, and yet I couldn't get away from him. It seemed as though certain forces were taking over. I hardly slept that night.'

The following day, Mitch took Sarah to visit the ruins of a castle. 'He kept talking about things like making yourself invisible by supernatural power, and seeing black shapes in the woods – things that were under the surface, what you'd call 'black magic'. There was a side to him I just didn't know about! I began to think to myself, *You stupid thing. What are you doing here? What have you got yourself involved in?* I began to feel quite weird – I can't describe it.

I took the coach back to Wakefield, but by the time I got halfway there it seemed as though I was losing my grip on reality. My head was in a state of total confusion – there was a real sense of disintegration in my mind. I didn't know what it was.'

Sarah did her best to get on with daily life as normal. 'I suppose, like human beings in general, you try to adapt to what is happening, no matter how weird it is. But from that day on, the sense of disintegration grew. I began to feel as though I didn't exist and other people weren't real. I had very odd dreams at night. I dreamt that I died and my body floated off. There was a general blurring of the boundaries between sleep and wakefulness.'

She stumbled along for the next three months, investing all her energy in trying to appear as sane as possible. 'I didn't tell anybody that I was actually hearing voices in my head. The voices – or, rather, one voice – was like someone mad ranting at me all the time. I thought, *Perhaps I'm going schizophrenic. Maybe this is what they call an audible hallucination.* But somehow there was a lot more to it than that. It felt deeply spiritual, like I'd given a part of my innermost being away to Mitch. Like I'd become really vulnerable, let something in and become subject to it.'

One morning Sarah awoke to find that the voice had stopped. She felt, somehow, that she was no longer fully present. 'It was as though I'd left my body. I didn't have any root – I was just this gas floating from place to place. My faculties of imagination simply weren't there. My mind was like a flat piece of paper with no depth to it. I didn't have much idea of time. I didn't know what day it was. I couldn't even remember how old I was, I had such a lack of a sense of myself.'

She went to see her family GP in the hope of obtaining

some sleeping pills. Much to her shock, he asked her if she'd ever been involved in the occult. On hearing her account, he instructed her to have nothing more to do with Mitch. 'For some reason, during this time, and especially after what the doctor said about the occult, I remembered that when I went to church as a child, as a Girl Guide, I'd heard about Jesus being the one who came to destroy the works of the Enemy. It wouldn't leave my consciousness. Fortunately, I knew that the woman who lived next door to my parents, Elsie, was a very strong Christian, so I went round there. She was really surprised to see me. I said, "I want to find Jesus. Can you help me find Jesus?" She kind of dragged me in and hugged me.'

Together with Elsie, Sarah began to attend the church she had once gone to as a Girl Guide. 'It was actually a lot more alive than I thought it would be. I could tell there were people there who had real experiences of God.' However, though she found the congregation warm and supportive, her condition did not improve over the next six months.

A friend suggested that there might be people at the church he was attending in Exeter, who could help her. One couple there, Mike and Amy, had a strong prayer and counselling ministry. Sarah travelled down to visit them. 'I spent one evening with Amy, and she just understood so much about what had happened to me. She knew it wasn't just a case of my "getting a job and then everything would be okay". She knew there was some heavy inner healing and spiritual deliverance needed.' Sarah made her decision: she would move to Exeter. Back in Yorkshire, she went to tell her vicar. He said, 'Before you go, I want to pray for you. It would be good to ask the Holy Spirit to come and fill you.'

'He got out some scented oil and anointed me with it. I closed my eyes. All of a sudden, I felt something like a waterfall coming down on my head. It washed right through my body and touched my spirit in a way that was so wonderful and refreshing, because I'd felt so locked up inside. I was crying my eyes out. I was so joyful, because it was the kind of evidence of God's power that I really needed to experience.'

She rented a room in Mike and Amy's house in Exeter. Here she was given structure for her days and regular prayer. It was June 1988. 'It was all very bleak, even after this experience of the Holy Spirit. I was still so zombie-like and detached. I kept pushing forward with my faith, but felt quite faint-hearted a lot of the time. I thought, *How do I know this is 'the Way, the Truth and the Life'?* I remember crying myself to sleep at night, still feeling this incredible desperation inside. People were praying for me to be set free from the powers of darkness, but it seemed like the drama of what they were doing didn't match up with what was happening in me. The Enemy really used that against me, saying, "You are wasting these people's time. They're just making idiots of themselves and nothing is going to happen." '

That autumn she moved into a new home with her brother and two friends. She also took on her first paid employment for over a year – a gardening vacancy came up. 'I got the job. It was beyond my belief, really. I'd read somewhere that people recovering from occult experiences should work with the creation, because there is something very healing about it. Roy, my boss, was just so caring, so nurturing and so gentle. I knew that it was provision from God.'

Nevertheless, Sarah reached a further point of despair

one evening during a church meeting. Everyone present gathered round to pray for her and, following this, a group met to pray specifically for her every Monday night. 'Again, there were some desolate times – times when, after a prayer session, I'd just go upstairs and get angry with God. A lot of people experience this. They so want to be healed, they so want to be out of the situation they're in, and yet it doesn't happen. Day in, day out, nothing changes. However, after a while, I did begin to feel a little more human.'

Sarah never thought she'd experience attraction to someone of the opposite sex again. 'I felt sexless. But one day I found myself singing old Fifties' love songs in the bath. I thought, *Who is this about?* Then I realised. The next day I went to work, I looked at my boss and I thought, *I really like this bloke*. Some normal feelings had come back! I didn't fancy my chances very much, but one thing led to another and we eventually got together.'

On a sunny August day in 1991, Sarah and Roy were married. Her parents and many of her friends were present. 'I just knew, again, that this was from God. I thought I was too broken to have a relationship, but this showed me otherwise. I had stability in my life and the healing was beginning to come through.'

Mitch, however, still seemed to have a hold over Sarah, despite the fact she had prayed to be freed from him. 'I'd see someone from behind and think it was him. It was like I was still looking for him. But it was more binding than that. I was praying with Amy one time, and I made a confession. I acknowledged my own stupidity, my ignorance and my sinfulness, the fact that I had just been following my desires when I got involved with him. Whatever he had done, whatever his girlfriend had done, I'd gone along with it. I told Jesus that, once and for all, I wanted to be cut off from him. It was a real battle to get the words out, but when we'd finished praying I felt such release. I cried with relief that I could finally walk away from him.'

She was worshipping God at a home group when a further breakthrough occurred. As Sarah sat on the floor, Amy prayed for her. 'All of a sudden, I started breathing heavily. There was something inside me which couldn't bear what she was saying. She was reading from the Book of Revelation, about how Satan would be consumed by fire and destroyed when Christ comes again. As she did so, I felt this terrible inner conflict, and then I was set free of whatever it was that was making me feel so afraid. During that year, I had a lot of very dramatic deliverance. Gradually, I got more and more released, and I began to experience a level of peace and confidence I hadn't known before.'

That Christmas, Sarah returned to Yorkshire and, together with Roy and her brother, she went to pray with Elsie. 'We were sitting around chatting, and this Taizé chant came on: "My peace I leave you, my peace I give you, trouble not your hearts." Those are the words Jesus spoke to his disciples – I think it was just before the crucifixion. But it wasn't like the voice of someone at Taizé singing; it was as if Jesus was saying those words to me. They are such simple words, but the impact of them was incredible. The truth of it permeated my heart, and I was just totally arrested by it. It was amazing!'

Epilogue

LOVE CHANGES EVERYTHING: AN EXPLANATION

These are the true stories of real people. They are just seven among millions of other stories that, together, form part of the grand, true story which began at the foundations of the earth and which is yet to reach its final chapter. You can read this great story in the Bible (from which all the following verses are taken); but it is still unfolding. The Bible continues to speak into people's lives, people like those whose stories are told here, echoing their emotions and transforming their circumstances. For example, the following psalm was written around 2,500 years ago, yet it still has resonance for Cherie, because it gives full expression to her state of mind during that traumatic period of her life:

> I love the LORD, because he hears me;
>> he listens to my prayers.
> He listens to me
>> every time I call to him.
> The danger of death was all round me;
>> the horrors of the grave closed in on me;
>> I was filled with fear and anxiety.
> Then I called to the LORD,
>> "I beg you, LORD, save me!"...

The LORD saved me from death;
  he stopped my tears
  and kept me from defeat.
(Psalm 116:1–4,8)

When we look around us, we can see that life seems like a huge contradiction, a bittersweet affair. On a good day, what a wondrous place the world is! The glinting constellations on a crisp winter's night. The pleasure of laughing at a TV comedy show. The love of our often insufferable family members! There are books to read, films to watch, friends to make, meals to savour, holidays to plan... The world is essentially a good place to be. God designed it that way.

How clearly the sky reveals God's glory!
  How plainly it shows what he has done!
Each day announces it to the following day;
  each night repeats it to the next.
No speech or words are used,
  no sound is heard;
yet their message goes out to all the world
  and is heard to the ends of the earth.
(Psalm 19:1–4)

From the sky you send rain on the hills,
  and the earth is filled with your blessings.
You make grass grow for the cattle
  and plants for human beings to use,
so that they can grow their crops
  and produce wine to make them happy,
  olive oil to make them cheerful
  and bread to give them strength.
(Psalm 104:13–15)

Yet in the midst of so many good things we cannot escape our own or other people's suffering. Like the sudden onset of Catherine's ME, we all face the possibility of illness and disease. New and old viruses threaten us despite the advances of medical science. Thousands take Prozac and other drugs to deal with depression. Eating disorders are common. Relationship problems like those experienced by Hans and Astrid, and other emotional traumas, fuel a heavy demand for counselling services. It is not just the elderly who encounter deep loneliness.

In societies across the world, there is increasing anxiety over rising levels of violent crime: its victims, like Cherie, often struggle long after events. Family breakdown troubles many. Racism persists year after year. We are sickened at the repeated abuse of the young placed in 'caring' institutions. We are stressed at work, as conditions become less secure in the global marketplace. We work long hours and, in the affluent West, shop as therapy for our troubles.

Cracks in the Antarctic ice shelves and coastal flooding have already resulted from global warming. The destruction of wildlife and plants continues to impoverish the world's environment. We are stunned by the horrific crimes committed against civilians in the heat of war, by the limbs and lives destroyed by landmines. The children of Iraq suffer under sanctions, the people of Russia under economic collapse, and the family members of the 'disappeared' experience a lack of justice in South America. Ernesto is still troubled by the unknown fate of some of his university associates in Peru.

The extent of human troubles seems overwhelming. And yet, looking back into history, we see that life has always been this way.

Then I looked again at all the injustice that
goes on in this world. The oppressed were
weeping, and no one would help them. No
one would help them because their
oppressors had power on their side. I envy
those who are dead and gone; they are better
off than those who are still alive. But better
off than either are those who have never been
born, who have never seen the injustice that
goes on in this world. *(Ecclesiastes 4:1–3)*

For we know that up to the present time all
of creation groans with pain, like the pain of
childbirth. *(Romans 8:22)*

Given this state of affairs, it is very difficult to live life
without a hope for a better life personally or nationally.
Some believe that technology will, in time, deliver all the
solutions we need: a NASA official at the launch of the
new multi-billion dollar space-station described it as a
'bright star of hope in the sky' for humanity. Others work
hard for sufficient money to retreat from the world
around them. Millions play the lottery weekly. For the
younger 'chemical generation', a tablet can neutralise reality at least for a night – a consolation that Robin was once
well acquainted with. Many others around the world hope
for the chance of life in any wealthy country, yet we know
the West is hardly paradise.

Then again, many of us may personally feel comfortable enough right now.

From the beginning of time God has always been at
work bringing healing to his damaged world. Ultimately,
he sought us through the person of Jesus Christ. Two

thousand years ago, this carpenter from the town of Nazareth in Palestine began teaching and healing the people who flocked to listen to him as he travelled round the region's towns and villages. His work had been foretold by Israel's prophets as one who would open God's arms to the whole world.

Jesus said of himself: 'I am the way, the truth, and the life; no one goes to the Father except by me ... Whoever has seen me has seen the Father' (John 14:6,9); 'I am the light of the world ... Whoever follows me will have the light of life and will never walk in darkness' (John 8:12); 'I am the bread of life ... Those who come to me will never be hungry; those who believe in me will never be thirsty' (John 6:35). Christians believe that Jesus is who he claimed to be – the Son of God. In Jesus, God became human and lived among us. In his teachings and actions, we see the character of God revealed in a way that no other wise man, prophet or philosopher, throughout all history, can show us: 'Christ is the visible likeness of the invisible God' (Col 1:15).

The gospel, or 'good news', is that there is a wide open door into the presence of God. If we go through it we will find life, peace and wholeness: 'I have come in order that you might have life – life in all its fullness' (John 10:10). Catherine experienced a foretaste of this life restored to her when she danced at her sister's wedding. This way of hope for our lives as individuals and communities is open only because of what Jesus Christ accomplished here. Our sinful nature – which separates us from God and which is evident in our abuse of his world, ourselves and each other – should have resulted in a just punishment of death. The scale of our sin through all history is unfathomable. But by his death by crucifixion, Jesus took our punishment upon his own back and laid down his life for us. This was the message revealed to Bob in his prison cell:

> Through the Son, then, God decided to bring
> the whole universe back to himself. God
> made peace through his Son's sacrificial
> death on the cross, and so brought back to
> himself all things, both on earth and in
> heaven. At one time you were far away from
> God and were his enemies because of the evil
> things you did and thought. But now by
> means of the physical death of his Son, God
> has made you his friends, in order to bring
> you holy, pure, and faultless, into his
> presence. *(Colossians 1:20–22)*

After his crucifixion, Jesus was raised from death. The resurrected Christ left the tomb victorious over death itself. This event shines out replete with the promise of a new life for us, both in this world and the next. There is no greater offer available to humanity, and it is an offer which you, the reader, can take hold of.

Before Jesus ascended into heaven, he commissioned his followers to tell the world about him. He promised that, after he left, the Holy Spirit would come in power to transform and to guide, to renew and to comfort all those who follow him. The accounts of all the stories in this book testify to this.

The Christian faith invites us to turn back to our loving Creator to find the hope and guidance we need. God is giving us time to turn back to him. His offer of forgiveness for our sins and a close relationship with him has been on the table for 2,000 years. It is there for each generation to embrace or reject.

Christians believe that Jesus Christ will return in power to judge the life of every individual. This judgement will be made in full knowledge of our circumstances: Jesus knows the opportunities and hardships we have experienced, the wrongs we have committed and how we have been wronged. The earth will be renewed and cleansed of evil and suffering and, from then on, life will be a complete and heavenly experience. Sarah saw her own life cleansed of evil and was given a foretaste of that all-embracing future peace.

But Jesus made it clear that not everyone would enter this paradise; only those who receive his saving love can be sure of it:

> 'Ask and you will receive; seek and you will
> find; knock, and the door will be opened to
> you. For everyone who asks will receive and
> anyone who seeks will find, and the door will
> be opened to those who knock.'
> *(Matthew 7:7–8)*

> I prayed to the LORD and he answered me;
>   he freed me from all my fears.
> The oppressed look to him and are glad;
>   they will never be disappointed.
> The helpless call to him and he answers;
>   he saves them from all their troubles.
> His angel guards those who honour the LORD
>   and rescues them from danger.
>
> Find out for yourself how good the LORD is.
>   Happy are those who find safety with him.
> *(Psalm 34:4–8)*

Here is a prayer you may like to use if you want to change the focus of your life and put God at the centre, restoring the intimacy with him which he wants every one of us to have.

> Lord God, you are great beyond all I can imagine. It's amazing that you care for me, yet I know it's true. You sent your Son to this world so that all the wrong I've done could be forgiven and I could be reconciled with you. Because Jesus died on the cross and rose again, I can know you as my Father.
>
> Lord God, only you can save me. I desperately need your forgiveness and your transforming power in my life. Please make me a new person, because I am trusting in Jesus. From now on, help me to want to please you in everything I do. Thank you that you have promised to hear and answer everyone who sincerely calls out to you. Amen.

FURTHER RESOURCES

If you want to find out more about Christianity, why not visit churches in your area and find out if they run 'seeker-services' or other events for people who are interested but not yet ready to commit themselves to the faith? Alternatively, you might like to contact the Christian Enquiry Agency (address below). CEA, a charity supported by all the major churches will send relevant literature and put you in touch with Christians in your area – but no one will call on you or phone you unless you specifically ask them to. Otherwise, the following resources may be of interest.

Alpha
A good introduction to the Christian faith is the popular Alpha course. You can find out more about this from local churches, or contact tel 0207 581 82555; web site: www.alpha.org.uk *Alpha News* contains a full register of the courses happening around the country. This is free and is published three times a year.

Scripture Union
Scripture Union can offer a number of resources which may be of interest:

RSVP: Discovering Jesus in John's Gospel by Peter Grant
For those wanting to discover more about Christianity, this booklet takes you through John's Gospel, offering guidance on becoming a Christian and getting started in the Christian faith. ISBN 0 949720 64 X, £1.50

Daily Bread for New Christians by Gillian Peall
Gives new Christians a biblical foundation to their faith
and helps them find the answers to questions like, 'What
does it mean to "follow Jesus" or "believe in him"?'
ISBN 1 85999 162 9, £2.00

What Now? First steps of Christian discipleship
A small booklet explaining how to become a Christian.
ISBN 0 85892 415 3, £1.50

To find out more about these and other Scripture Union
resources, contact 207–209 Queensway, Bletchley, MK2
2EB; tel 01908 856006; fax 01908 856020.
Email info@scriptureunion.org.uk
Or visit our website: www.scriptureunion.org.uk

Christian Enquiry Agency
CEA (SU1)
FREEPOST
SE 5940
LONDON
SE1 7YX
email: enquiry@christianity.org.uk

Web sites
There are a vast number of Christian web sites, some better than others. You may like to check out the following:

www.hopenet.net
www.biblesearch.com
www.christianity.net.au
www.christianchat.co.uk
www.greenbelt.org.uk